T0051723

Cantadora — Letters from California
Linda Ravenswood

Cantadora —
Letters from California

Linda Ravenswood

THE **BLACK SPRING**
PRESS GROUP

First published in 2023
An Eyewear Publishing book, The Black Spring Press Group
Grantully Road, Maida Vale, London W9
United Kingdom

Typesetting User Design, Illustration and Typesetting, UK
Cover art Linda Ravenswood, photo collage, (photograph of Mitla, Oaxaca, México,
   c.1874, no attribution, & Johann Jacob Scheuchzer, Fenestrae Coeli Apertae, 1731) 2023

The author has requested the publisher use American spelling
and grammar wherever possible in this edition

All rights reserved
© Linda Ravenswood 2023

The right of Linda Ravenswood to be identified as author of
this work has been asserted in accordance with section 77
of the Copyright, Designs and Patents Act 1988

ISBN-13 978-1-913606-24-4

to the ghosts & the letter writers

Contents

Autumn   67
Pipe Dream Planet

Winter
The Long Trip Home

Land acknowledgment

i acknowledge that my home & birthplace in California exists upon the occupied territory of hundreds of Indigenous tribes. This homeplace has been stewarded by our Indigenous ancestors since time immemorial.

i acknowledge the Gabrielino & Tongva peoples as the traditional stewards of Tovaangar (the unceded territory of Los Angeles).

i acknowledge the land & the water. i acknowledge that tribal continuity & community preservation depends upon clean, shared, secure & sustainable land & water access.

i acknowledge the history upon which the state of California has been built, how policies, systems, & structures of spoken & unspoken racism, oppress & erase People of Colour.

i honor & respect the history of the original inhabitants & places that preceded the founding of Los Angeles & i am committed to sharing this history in my work.

i am committed to continuing the work of kinship, listening, support, & reparation as well as building long-lasting relationships with Indigenous & other community partners.

i am grateful to work for the taraaxotam (Indigenous peoples) & for their continuing flourishing, security & safety.

i offer thanks & homage to our shared Honuukvetam (Ancestors), elders, & 'Eyoohiinkem (our relatives/relations) past, present & on their way.

Foreword

Cantadora — Letters from California by Linda Ravenswood delivers multitudinous escapades, with ins and outs of being in the world with fixed and shifting perimeters. It speaks to Being Mixed with luminous medley. It is a ricochet of childhood seasonings where the speaker,

> *fervently worshipped the tiger inside my mouth*,

then matures to interrogating codified switch terming, Hispanic/Latino, whereas

> *Hispanic means white (ish) // Turn down service. Sugar cube //*

countering;

> *Sometimes when you're Latino, you long to be the bear.*

In rising suites of anaphora —

> *praise their breath & fingertips on the hearth //*
> *praise their diffidence // praise their strength*

Ravenswood invokes us to follow her, leading us through familial journeys; love, reckonings, griefs.

Through California and across the country on rambling journeys, always under constellations where the bear and archer fulfil human notions of sky and hover awaiting what becomes of us, this book is a collection of visceral impulse - negotiating identities, congenital and claimed, leaving us with

> *Hold hands with me in dreams // & let us sing a while //*
> *some soft-strung words*

as a measure of something glorious midst the everyday. A beautiful book, a full rapture. These letters are the heartbeat of California.

Allison Adelle Hedge Coke,
Distinguished Professor of Literature, University of California, Riverside
Creative Writing, School of Medicine,
Dept. of Environment, Sustainability, & Health Equity (ESHE)

Author's Note

The editors of this collection have asked me to offer a few words of clarification regarding Intersectionality. Much of the work in *Cantadora — Letters from California* involves sensitive topics surrounding race, ethnicity, & issues of *passing** & belongingness.

As a person of mixed parentage, i honour & revere the multitudes of histories that have shaped my vision, built my arts praxes, & continue to influence my work. While i am by no means an expert in Indigeneity, i affirm that i devote my entire career to working against the erasure of history, most especially of the Indigenous peoples & WIPOC of California.

i acknowledge the 500th anniversary of the Conquest of Mexico (1521–2021), the ensuing Spanish colonial period, plague, genocide, failed treaties of US govts., relocations & removals of peoples, dwellings, sacred sites, businesses, & places of learning of Indigenous Peoples from both sides of the US/Mexico border. These systems perseverate. These sensitive subjects are engaged in *Cantadora — Letters from California*.

Other sensitive topics include the Holocaust, sexual assault, eating disorders, drug addiction.

i work within the framework of the emergence of a whole, now mixed, cultural entity of Mestizaje, further enriched by Judaism. These new/old cultures of multiple commonalities, of intersections, & an ultimate union of shared vision, populate the work. As an artist of converging ethnic & cultural identities, i resonate within a richly cross-pollinated methodology. i acknowledge the work of Clarissa Pinkola Estes, Elizabeth Martinez, Gloria Anzaldua, Ana Mendieta, Theresa Hak Kyung Cha & others.

Shared history compels me to parry & move within these legacies. The poems in *Cantadora — Letters from California* take action to interrupt the whip of colonialism & genocide, & to redress erasures, challenges, injustices, & prejudices leveled at WIPOC (Women & Indigenous People of Colour), & especially Indigenous peoples. For centuries, tribal & Indigenous communities have been dispossessed of ancestral lands.

---

*   *passing* refers to a happenstance of appearing traditionally White, or European, though one might be a person of colour, or a person of mixed parentage. In cases of passing, it might behoove one to be mindful of access afforded in matters of hegemonic cultural opportunities, & work towards uplifting others so that all people may have the occasion to flourish.

To displace Indigenous peoples & communities of colour from homesteads, neighbourhoods, & opportunities in the emerging metropolis, is criminal & heinous. Further compounded by polarities of disaffection & half-hearted invitation (while at the same time forcing assimilation), these injustices serve to erase cultures & identities.

i am committed to working alongside other WIPOC, & allies especially those indwelling Chicana, Mestiza, and communities of Latinidad & Indigeneiety at the intersections of art, literature, & discourse. Much of the writing in *Cantadora — Letters from California* speaks to a negotiation of *between-ness*.

SPRING
To the Sweat & the Breath

all the bells of Mare Island

Mother's lungs. the way they slip in view on the x-ray screen. shoe & shoehorn. a soft
satin bray against some Pacific Coast her body. nights full of stars my grandfather
holding her up & in & out of weeks so she would not die from whooping cough. his warm
Scots-Irish hands against her back. the soft clothes of the 1940s all the bells of Mare Island
& fog along the Farallones. it was the second world war & the rubber drive. their
house-on-wheels all the way from Oregon so my grandfather could wire sonar
for the ships in San Francisco Bay. they pulled together to get into the black her lungs
so scarred some San Andreas Fault lines her veins. they said she would pull through
for what for what for what

Esther Wigotski

Esther Wigotski was the sister of Henry Kress. & Henry Kress & his wife
Mary Kress were survivors of the Holocaust capital H. Esther Wigotski
was a handsome woman in her 50s when I knew her. She had that hair
the women of the 1970s wore from their time in other decades. Choked curls
& blonde. & dirty blonde. & folded. & oiled & draped on the face. Lipstick
in the kind of coral pink the 1970s brewed. The kind of colour
found on food & sauce & ladies restrooms. The kind of colour
that came from inside the radio. Cough syrup & ballet ribbons.
A kind of colour that makes a girl say *I love pink   pink is my colour*.
The kind of pink that trails with you ever after.   Esther Wigotski
came to events & shabbats & dinners & weddings. She wore strappy-back
high-heeled sandals on dark / nude pantyhose & knee length diaphanous skirts
with ruffle hems. She had brown knuckles & clacking rings. She had money
& a new Dodge. Her husband was rotund & grey with starched long collared shirts
but Esther Wigotski had been a Capo in the camps so even though people smiled
as they passed her tea, when she lowered her eyes they whispered   *bitch*.

California girl watches all the Jews of Los Angeles knowing she is on the outside
looking in. Knowing she is no blood relation.   Knowing she is listening, some
keep her out. Some draw her close Aunt Judy & Uncle Paul Skopitski squire her
around Palo Alto gardens all the trees they planted with their bare hands & 5 dollars
in their pocket *when first we came to United States we brought the plum tree*
it was the size of a house cat look now & here my kumquat we never had in Poland
look now its berries go above the roof sometimes in wind I hear fruit dancing
on the shingles & know there is a G-d

1519 water dream

Chontales people on the cliffs of Yucatán see Cortes' ships approaching, north of Tlapaco.
They imagine these 'ship structures' as floating houses, hovering towards land.
Perhaps land itself imagines   —
Perhaps animals wonder.

1

It's 1519.
I'm a Bird.

    I with my I

see with my eye
say with my eye

2

    desert

3

    .....

4

look —
    a chunk
    on water —
flowing —
following —

5

stalking —

6

it comes to
rest on the desert —
a house
coming
on water —
a piece —
missing of its own tongue
    frontera
     drags
along the bottom
   jettisons the ocean
as it slides

look now —

7

a piece
boiling on the water

8

a House-on-water

9

I'm a bird
I know this desert
   a falcon
    returning home
   a bird turning —
it cannot be all bad
a bird must turn in the desert
to give birth to many brothers
& apple trees

10

what new language I speak —
    plastic in the throat
    of water birds.
                some evolution —
tell all   your friends
I'm   home

11

who holds the paper here
ask that bunch of Indios over there
who holds the title
andale, lo mismo
I see ..... a hotel —
do you see it ..
Imagine it

12

it's 1519
i am a bird

Data is extremely limited, amounting
only to four words & ten place names.

    x   ]\ tehat ichtli

[[Data   is   extremely   limited
amounting   only
to   four   words
&   ten   place   names.]]

       these are the words of my people. (Maybe.
or maybe
I'm just a witness.)
      a fourth cousin, twice removed.
      (the shapes
      that blood can lean-to.
      ~~if your mouth does not say //~~
      ~~if your face is turned from the sun.~~

these are the words of my people. (Maybe.)

    Aiñiní: the location of the uptop Misión —
    the sound
    of interlopers
       where they hang their hats.
            evening
the sound of a new idea
on an old place //
some new thing
on the tone of desert.

it refers to others //
   distant daughter
   how do you say your name

Anicá: a Pericú settlement
a settlement &
not a town
you can only have a polis
    if you are white
      or   part white
      or   possess tooth
    and   mettle
    to make   a wall of wire
       only   then   will   sides   be worthy
come
    build my nation
you of no nation
come
    raise up my children
you who have
    some   litters
&   tribes
    make a palanquin of your culture   & ride me everywhere.

Añuití — the location of the other Mission
San José del Cabo
i am looking for you
by the nettles
i saw you one time
hermano

**Caduaño — a location in the modern city of Los Cabos — *green
arroyo***
the desert is dry
except it is not

Calluco
the desert is green
a name
    for the people
    i make a mark in

clay

    to say

        i remember this place
        i come from its bushes & sky

Cunimniici — a mountain range
the teeth of the mountain
guide me home
after waking dark places

Eguí
father calls me
& i turn
to the place he made
for the people to dance

Marinó — the Santa Ana Mountains
i lay my head on the clay bundle
i become
something that is not vanished

Purum — a group of mountains & a Pericú settlement
it is a town
& a purpose
you
    could meet
your mother there
&
    help her
carry your brother

Yeneca — a Pericú settlement
my hands wash you
the ash   cleans you
you are coming   into the homeland

Yenecamú — Cabo San Lucas
interloper in the blue
intruder   desert scallion
(a daughter is not an impostor)
    (witness this whiteness)
this cavern
glows by night   & noon
the living gather here
        singer   walker   (we come)

miñicari — **sky**
all about me
all above
in my eyes & blood

unoa — **give**
i will run to you
across rivers & champions
i will sing to you in ages
& never forsake
such a place
& song

utere — **sit**
when   we   are   come   home

Venice, 1982

I

my grandmother   had a key   to an apartment in Venice.
in the 1980s   in her 70s   she'd go   under the breeze
to meet a man from the flea market.   a 1940s girl
still on active-duty.   victory curls   & Dippity Doo.
the clean ocean liners of her arms.

II

her teeth had fallen out in Portland Oregon.
grandmother's grandmother
gave her a dollar coin   for the dentist off Marguerite.
one by one.   year by year.
1919. 1922.   extractions.
when her mother's sister   would come-in after a date
she'd nudge my gran awake   *Dot, here's a sweetie*
& she'd lightly wake   to nest the chocolate
in her mouth   & go back to sleep.
   all night long in Portland Oregon
   she swelled that cocoa blossom
   to the end of dreams.

III

100 years ago
my grandmother lost her hearing in Portland Oregon.
a cold winter.
      if she was driving
      & her window was down
      you'd have to *speak-up*
      because her left ear
      was the good one
      & in the car
      all she could hear
      was the wind

IV
100 years ago
my grandmother's feet moved in sandals
along the earth.   yellow poplars.
she pressed the accelerator
& her car would drive
& drive.

V
how to construct an image
of a person long gone.
(not so long.   snowdrift in relation to planet.)
    for whom do we build these images.
                an answer resounds —
                        for us. ourselves in the wind.
                        the wind who is our brother
                            in the cold, black night.
                        the stillness of white sheets.
                    these are for whom the poem belongs.
                    to the sweat & the breath.
                    a poem belongs to the struggle

VI
Portland Oregon 1923.
my grandmother's grandmother builds a coat
with the formality of 19th century hands.
the dignity of a plumber's grand-daughter
in the early 1920s.   *Portland Oregon.*
the coat held military, baroque people who came across Waters.
Green Bay Wisconsin. memory of farmland.
white flowers in sepia.   a dog on a high wooden porch.
a dog in a field.   a dog under a house.   faces of children.
boys in hats on old farm equipment.   a tractor in sunlight.
these things surged in this coat
& more.   even at 10 years old
my grandmother recognized the pattern.
inhabited it.
    what part of it did she remember
    or forget as she walked from school.
    was it her lungs.   her teeth.

was it raining.   was it spring.
was it her ear —
she took a corner of the coat
& folded it in her hands.
a leek being prepared for wax paper.
preparing to go under.
she placed it through the eye
of the chain-link.
a holy host. she pushed.
breath in a vaulted mouth.

a gallery of yellow goats
received the weft
back to their family,
their brains.   they chewed
the scutch corners
of grandmother's grandmother's coat —
an ominous Mobius-strip of lambswool.

VII
when she came in
my great grandmother
saw the coat in shreds.
gran told her
      the goats were hungry & I fed them

VII
95 years later
I read
about a goat's head —
      severed & hanging in trees —
                  not immobilised
but singing its mystery.
      it was then I knew
poetry is genetic.

poem.   civilisation fund act 1819

I went to a school called army house.
in   the   morning   *yessir*   would   sit   at   table
a wooden altar covered in a vinyl tarp
of goldenrod flowers.   *yessum*   would lay down
his cloth napkin & spoon.   *yessir*
would sit
at angle   on the good chair   legs
crossed
reading folded newsprint.   he had
eyeglasses
hugging the bridge of his nose
tight as a dog muzzle / a yellow beetle /
        a bud poking through /
the beginning of an antler.
when   I   arrived   to   the   barely   lit   kitchen
yessum   would   point   with   her   chin   to   the wall
—

a square piece of paper & wax pencil on a string.
every day   she'd say   *write your birthday*
then a dash   then today's date.   at army house
this is focus.   prepare
for comings & goings.   study on the controllable
& the uncontrollable.   always say the name of the day
at army house.   i told her
my   birth day
is   in the moon of the popping trees.
she said   *write it the way i told you.*
            & then she did the dishes.

31

If I was smart as an onion skin

If I was smart as an onion skin
they wouldn't have gotten to me
they might have smelled me
but they wouldn't have gotten
inside.   I'd have kept my coat on
& they wouldn't've dared break it open
my loud onion skin coat
would've rattled down their hands
& instead of trying to pull it off
they'd've been trying to keep it quiet
& straight.   If I was an onion smart girl
I wouldn't've shown them my green secret
& my ruffle fringe.   I'd have
smiled with my whole face around
& they never would have seen the end of it.

Springtime 1

When I was a child
I fervently worshipped the tiger inside my mouth;
parted lips, geographic tongue,
all Indus Valley —
til my mother thrashed me in green grass
& smashed me in the cradle, screaming
wake up brown girl, it's spring.

I scrubbed my knuckles red as brown
could be (which is pretty red)
& saw that I was passing.
At the bus stop in Century City
I stood relieved
but little by little my hips & breasts
throbbed golden brown
& everyone up the block
huffed *gimme some.*   older girls
pushed me down —
breath on my lashes.
Little did I know the female gaze
& its blood-dark desire.
I was in my loops —
barbie & the jacaranda
so I kept my knees closed
though an ocean was jetting through.

& there my mother saw me.
swollen doing cartwheels
on her Mayflowers out front.
get a better bra for those pendulous breasts
she clobbered as still
I was too native for her spring.
She put up a bounty up that read
drop the brown
you're packing on
& all this will be yours

& glued the recipe
inside my eyelids.
I woke up
thick as ever
& she was gone.
Had you seen the tiger inside my mouth
you'd've worshipped too.
Finally, I inked up my eyebrows
& came fully to the Mendieta.
& the tiger lives on.

In right angle over deep waters

On a boat I could write. / On Vermilion Ocean
a poem would rise.   The green
sea tha falls in   & out   for hours
would find words for me. /
A map would rise.   The saddle of a fish.
Right angle bent & straining off the side of boat /
my watery face   low in salt water /
ancestor mirror / Vermilion Ocean.
On a boat   we are   a man   wandering /
pushed by eye & limb & weather.
If we had a dog   we would know how to walk.
& sing. / A man on a boat with a dog singing.
If we weren't shuttered / summer ragged
snatched indoors / we could feel
the difference between poems   & lists.
& poems & love letters.
gentle absurd differences
between poems   & hieroglyphs.
But this season / this whitest land.   Leaves
on puddle water / our unused driveway.
Telephone cinctures. / A tin of beans
painstakingly grown / never to be eaten.

When you're *Latino*

Hispanic means white (ish)
Unless you're white
then Hispanic means *I don't see you.*
'This land was your land for
how many years, *what*?'
'There was gold found, *where*?'
'... Can we .. eat it?'
'I want to wear gold
.. on the inside.'
'I want to be
that white.'

Hispanic means white (ish)
Turn down service. Sugar cube.
Private school.
Hispanic means Papa
owns a restaurant. Hispanic means Passing.

Latino means *Cholo.*
Indio.   Teardrop tattoo.
Latino means
stopped by the cops.
Probable flunk out, at least one grade.
Latino is embattled.   Splinters along *la lengua de nopal.*
Latino puts Xes on the ends of things
to call itself into existence.
Latino wants to be feared.

When you're Latino
you work the kitchen.
Latino means
hands of the business
not the face.

When you're Hispanic you go to medical school.
Smile at Ballet Folklórico.
(Don't forget to send a check.)
When you're Hispanic
you glance lovingly, but remotely
at Cultural Markers.   (Quaint. Simple.)
When you're Hispanic
there's a room in your house with indigenous masks on the wall.
People think you're a cultural torchbearer.
Nothing bad will happen to you.

When you're *Latino*
finishing high school
means you're a sellout
to some of your friends.
Oye Carnal.   Be Fierce.   Be hard.
Wear defiance like blue eyeshadow.
When you're *Latino*
you have grease under your nails —
Car, Lawnmower, *Comida.*
When you're *Latino* you make your eyebrows high and dark.
When you're *Latino*
you navigate *wet back* no matter how many smart clothes you wear.
Even your grandfather, *Tres Flores* slapped on both sides of his face
even he cannot escape *el olor.*

When you're Hispanic you have a library.
People come to dinner.   (Wine, flowers.)
You're well-liked. White people even
bring their babies when red spots appear in the night.
Dr. Lopez will know, he's lived here so long.
When you're Hispanic
they tell you
how much integrity you have
como las montañas, but
there is no earth to touch your cuffs
no bent back or leatherneck
from harvesting on your hands and knees.

When you're *Latino* there is A Book
at the bottom of your closet
near your shoes & suitcase.
Sometimes you look at The Book,
at The Seven Sisters Rising
forming a great marker
to the heavens to escape
the bear your brother has become.

Sometimes *Latino*
longs to be the bear.
Mostly *bebe birria*
y hangs in the window.
Boils about how it's *all Mexico*
how everything was swiped
while we were *grinding corn*
& building the whole city.

As a mostly white person in the time of why

How to lean into your Latinidad
if you were raised
by white people & Ashkenazi Jews /
how to find the way /
in the sweet loaded kitchen
of all Holocaust survivors.   Little h Big H.
Black Irish girl seeped in Mexican brine
& Litvok candy / how to
lean into your Latini/dad if you
don't understand / only trailing some epigenetic
centres of the universe
in blood & bones / all the ache & shame
around the city / indigo splotches
across your backside / wetback
right-in-the-face of 14 //
how did he know /
ain't my white privilege available in this light? /
how to understand Latini / dad
never having been to a quinceañera

  What is that cultural adjacency
  so close it might as well
  bear another ZIP Code, live in another part
  of the Thomas Guide, so far beyond
  the borders of recognition, red
  lined from the community chest //

your father drives up in his Cortés Gold
Cadillac fresh from *Burbank*
to give you a present
you cannot use
that you do not want /

  a shapeless / shadow / bucket-seat dwelling drinking buddy
  / you remember him right mija /
  / hi Linda /

/ *happy birthday* /
sits in the car.
pastel lemon lurches
a 1980s
colecock'd smear
against concrete /
then
pulls away //

yrs later men leave like this
peel off like this /
memories of distant strangers
all planet groaning
halted love affairs
in mirrors
where objects appear closer
than irl /

there in a throbbing vision cut
from some world of fatherishness
he ascends & recoils in clicktrack
golf clubs banging /
Diego Rivera /
bales of Canebrake /
bales of white lilies
a dondé vas papá ?
where are you going / LatiniDad?

/////Papa /////////////////////////////////////
//
// Papá /

The refugees come like monarchs

The soft bigotry of low expectation, sit down back
there, you're dead, in swaddling, hasta los huesos,
you are subtlest shadows, shhhhhhh

we're standing in our night gowns
parkas on, holding suitcases & plastic bags.
i re+member.
refugees come like
monarchs, our packs & crowns
toes in desert silt —
a bone, a ragged bit —
a jaw, a cup, my people.
we are here & home & gone
with winds on our frames
to bless
this pilgrimage, our
sky.

a woman with a two hand clap means food —
a two handed slap breeds our flat & filling meal —
flat song, teeth smiling, extruding corn meal
across ocean, tortuga belly
full of vegetables, dipping
a handmade scoop in simmering flesh —
the best meal you never had —
sand kicking its lashes for grit.
being Refugee means all this is yours —
golden singing to the black
crepe night, stars our microphones & mirrors.

i walk this desert
talk out the side of my mouth —
it's not cowardice
it's passing

don't see me white boy
you & ten like you —
don't see me
horde of mopeds on the low turn —
don't see this wet soul.
let me go on passing.
your ancient culture / my ancient culture /
can't we all just get along /

thunder boy butts come down hard /
a steely armature building civilisation /
smouldering cig curlers in labial folds /
i thought i could make it to town
& somewhere
in one of these white flats
a mother must be
caressing her kindergartener
& boiling a hissing sausage
that sings like me
all this grass on my tongue

children following their father through the house.

children following their father through the house.
the sound of his robe   as it swishes.   great wings
between sleep & morning coffee.   dungarees   crumpled
behind doors & daughters.   boys hide their father
through the house.   late night races   on the shoulders of dawn.
a course visited   on the neck of the son.   *locus poenitentiae*.
the sheet cape behind them.   suddenly
& not remotely   the sun's shoulders bend
against news of the father.   same arches.
same moves.   the way father lands
on the son.   doubtless oranges   on their tongues.
a father shines his song   against the blade of a boy.

SUMMER
The Nautilus Within

Response to *Dogs chasing my car in the desert* by John Divola

Contemplating a dog chasing a car.

it's possible   on   a   template   of   desert
a hollow wind can become a dog.
                a whole flash of head
into hooves.
                a dog   a horse   a mountain.
flights of gypsy tires.   stripes

of   flags   &   tongues.
paws are enough   for magic   in the desert.

a tourniquet   roped on a barge.

a desert   becomes a dog.   fast flowers   of dog mouths.
run-down by-houses.   a dirigible   on half-sped dog legs.

silver paws
never needed   hoof   or jaw.

a dog is enough for a desert.

speeding   on sand   a dog   can carry us home.

Praise when you like but mostly when children slam the door

Praise when you like but mostly when the children slam the door.
Remember. The glorious kitchen door of their youth
The kitchen door that says *the children are home*
the slamming door that says *we're still together*
the slamming door that says *someone's in the bathroom*.
praise the tubes that carry the bodily fluids of the children still at home.
Praise the pipe. Praise the water from the municipal government
& the water tenders who measure
so children can come through the house
like Clydesdales to pee in their family bowl.
Praise the history of the family loo on the corner in Glendale California
praise the slamming door that clocks you every two hours
from the children still in your house.
Praise the stone cutters & the stone & boulder rollers.
praise the Masons & carpenters who laid the foundation
to build the old craftsman houses of Los Angeles.
Praise the back generations we cannot know
that we know intrinsically
as we walk their planks & enter through their doorways
praise their breath & fingertips on the hearth
praise their diffidence
praise their strength
their work ethic
their good sense to leave & let us live
their tenacity
their history
praise the steel cutter
praise Homewood
praise Detroit
praise the janitor at the church
praise the sus volunteer at the school drop off
praise her bitchy face & bossy fingers
praise her forever

this message has no body

& if they took away your iPhone your helper your slave
that which enslaves others that you use with so much
oblivious gratitude which means America / would you still
be you & if they took away your rented house in a rented
part of town because your parents didn't believe in you
enough for a down payment on a piece of the dream /
would you still be you & if they took away your car the one
that was better than the other so you had to sleep in
the car that was the lesser of two evils / would you still be you
& if they took away your high-heeled shoes / your Fendi
bag & all your deodorant & you shambled streets &
hobbled hello to strangers faces / meal tickets & brine /
wondering where running water lives / would you still be you
& if they took away your children / your friends
or anyone who knew your name / given & carried all these years
showing it like a deck of cards at a carnival shell game / between
who you are & how you ache / seamstress of prostitutes &
taxi drivers / crock pot whistleblower / former endless cocksucker
mid-life failure / nameless in the city of names / would you still be
you & if they took away your sight so all you had was
the breeze when the breeze if the breeze & the sound of
pigeon on pavement / would you still be you & if they took
away all the skin of you / your wax paper show / your outer coating /
your reviled worst name / would you still be you?

Poetry is a Shapeshifter

Poetry must be a singer.
To remain relevant
Poetry must be liquid.
It must penetrate many crevices of society
present itself in many genres
& on many platforms
raise its head from traditional ideas
modes & venues
cling within the souls of the artists
& race to merge with the souls of the People —
it must be unafraid
bold. Poetry must sing.

Poetry must embrace multidimensionality
& multi-genre-ality
be liberal, but fierce in its disciplines
must have a champion
speak history
be indiscreet
tactless, falling down stairs like a toddler
slipping into ravines like a dancer on high alert
forgetting the words but remembering the way.
Poetry must be improvised from years of preparation
must be improvised from the genetic memory
Poetry must be.
Poetry must be.

Poetry must be politic
must have muscles
must bend low to serve the People
not just aggrandize the poet.
Poetry must have a big heart
& a great sense of humour
must travel light but bring with it
invisible cables of lineage, culture
resistance, & resilience.

The poet must speak for everyone —
her duty not to factions —
she should know the Tongva, the Gabrielino
the Mexican, the Spanish —
should not speak for only
one segment of the population
but for The German, The Irish
The Jewish, The Hmong
The Japanese, The Ethiopian, The Laotian.
The poet should speak from the depths of poverty
& from the hope of a just wealth —
from the streets & the salon

The poet's hair
if she has hair
her arms, if she possess them
her eyes
if they be
must belong to her
though they be recycled
from a hundred other sources.
From these vessels & others
she must give nourishment to a People.

The poet should know the land.
She should understand Chavez Ravine
& Dodger Stadium & speak with mercy & generosity
towards both civic realities.
She must stretch imaginations —
causes, firmaments, & destinies
to search out justice
amendments, reparations
forgivenesses, concords
& ultimate brother & sisterhood
She must not be pigeonholed by politics
but use politics to resound fervent truths
to share place & to re + member hope

The poet must understand the complexities in history
yet be not bound only

by their sacred facts & feelings.
The poet must be led by the ominous possibilities
of universal evolution —
light new imaginings for change
sing towards new roads
forge new alliances & even new friendships from broken promises.

The poet should live here
in this gloriastic chasm
somewhere between student & teacher
shaman & servant, magician & fool.
The poet must dance here —
& bow to all dissemblers & non believers —
must perseverate when others pack up their rags & go home
must stand in the dark
& wait on her own dime
her own frayed edges —
must cry, but never give out —
longer & stronger, Chiron
searching endlessly for salves —
the objects & means of healing

Because poetry must sing:
it must embrace the Russian, the Italian
the Yemeni, the Congolese
must stand, voiced
& supported by the ancestors
comfortable in boardroom or soup kitchen
ready in classroom, breathless on an aeroplane
perched on the back of a tractor, dancing
at a used car lot, waiting in the wings, or praying
in an old bus station.

Poetry must mean these things
& be these things
& make these things
& honour these things
with-out a shred of pandering
& with all her heart.

We must travel light but travel like lightning —
must bring the force of light with us
have stamina, strength, hope
vigilance, sight —
must be able to speak from the memory of place
through personal trauma, for untapped dreams
only dared in crossed fingers & quick breaths.

It is essential that the poet be a mixed person
maybe even dropped on her head once or twice —
maybe her father left
or stayed but couldn't speak
& another language had to be met
maybe her mother was a circus rider
or she went to the pictures instead of Calculus
maybe her teeth were knocked in
or she lay in Orthopaedic Hospital all of 3rd grade
or saw a man beaten on a corner
out of the corner of her eye
& she never dis-remembered —
It is essential that the poet live in that liminal place
toward wholeness of humanity

If the poet can be a person of multiple heritages
with allegiances to all
If the poet can be college-educated
If the poet can be someone who experiences prison
If the poet can be a world traveller
a seamstress
a high school dropout
If the poet can live out of their car
or on the beach

If she knows Dante's Trail, the Magic Castle
the Paleteros in Boyle Heights
Hop Louie's, the Saugus Cafe
Llano del Rio, Geoffrey's in Malibu & Mitrice Richardson
Angels Flight, the Red Car, The La Brea Tar Pits
The Farmers Market before The Grove
Ray Bolger's dance at Good Shepherd Church

Wrightwood at dawn, what the Third Street
Promenade looked like before 1995
where Tony Curtis filmed in Los Feliz
the California Incline
Leimert Park & The World Stage
when you could swim Santa Monica Bay
the South Central Farm

If the poet can know
If the poet can remember
If the poet can sing
If they can be an old man & a young woman
If they can be an old woman & a young man
because
Poetry must be.
Poetry must be.

The Saint of Memory

The Peas

She came from the West
where rain
measures the hours
in drops
against the house —
where land
breaks
into great crags
along the coast of water.
Her high
gothic façade of radio
hollowly sings
through the sitting room
where she's been waiting
against the window panes;
it's raining
down the garden rows
& the trellis
is beating the overhang
like a metronome.
Apples sweat
in the lane
above the soaking smudge pots,
in the beds
the lettuce leaves
are ripped & drizzling.
Mushrooms bauble
in the mud
but *the peas* —
she says against the panes
the peas are safe.
In their fibre boats
they're lolling
in the trickle

such greenness un-muted
by the wash.

In the dawn of that day
she flung some out
of their shells
sweetly plinking to a bowl —
a ghostly memorandum of spring.
The house was clean & agile then
the basins white-shining
& the wood well-rubbed.
1930 in the fall
was before money & moving —
her people were plumbers & farmers
but she married well
& took to tea
& touring cars.

I never knew her that way;
as she was ageing
she sloughed superfluous finery
& became an Oregonian —
old & mindful in the window.

In the dusk of that day
she was so old
in her bed —
her daughters about her
against the tapestries
like Bayeux matrons.

There in the spinning,
I saw that even in
death she was more alive
than those stiff keeners.
She was real
& oaken
& pirating the bed.

She was tilting
& wet but she managed
to say
her words

put me where the peas are

& she was fast away.

In the years beyond
I pull them
from the bins
at the market —
green & wonderful.
They're holy,
these slim
vegetables
a legacy of will
a trust of spirit
endowing more than
any stick of Louis Quatorze
or stretch of oil.
They're of the good
lathery soil.
Like her —
green & sure
forward in the window —
watching the garden in the rain
long ago days
when she was living
with her whistle
& her custard
& her canvas shoes.

We did this on earth —
Triptych

(1)
We did this on earth. Made a crown. Chauvet light.
Shelved a border. Had a diet. Had a bath.
Penile insertion. Had a laugh. Had a baby.
Built a wall. Built a church. Cried to sleep. TransAtlantic wire.
Dropped a bomb. Had a drink. Lamented.
Took the host. Swallowed hard, hopefully
rubbed knees – wiped lips. Another baby.
Saw Rhodesia. Hurricanes of popular uprising held/failed.
Kings marbled paper & testicular mapping. Ho-hum.
Slugged all manner viscous fluids. Fingers. Hands. Pubic longings.
School days forgotten, remembered later. Lied.
Wanked off in Ibiza. Climbed Masada. Never knew my father. TV.
Burned apples & the smoke told them we were here.
Went to the island.
Longing for home, confused, culture shocked
we left on the ship in the bay;
slip staring out over the gangway
just in time, starting out, arms pressed
against the bannisters, watched our town disappear sliding off a rock
light bulbs exploding, the wood well-rubbed, Ireland
whatever you call it, what was this marriage
who were we, our feet into grass, moss
hands in loss, an eternity of peat
who were we there, then, where did you go when you died.
All the windows that day

(2)
We did this on earth —
cried & cried &
cried & fingered
mud clods wondering
if they were diamonds
or just ragged histories —
all water returning.

Filtered in over everyone memories
blankets, bed rolls, Teepees
all the wanderings like Jews in deserts
freshman road trips across a jagged map.
We did this on earth —
beerbongs & spaghetti straps
fuckt her behind a dumpster
thought no one saw. Tryna be the greatest
on the swim team & in the mirror at night
talk myself up hard, wank off & cry
& cry & cry myself to sleep.
No mother. This track record follows me
wherever I go, Starbucks, on the cots in swept out barracks
doing faux army games. Retreat. Everywhere
all the turned-over earth
all the Mexicans along
the side of the berm
waiting for someone
to pick them up
like recycling boys
on Santa Monica Blvd.

we can't disappear
even if we want to

(3)
We did this on earth-
opened a fallow sack
on the way to Reforma —
son of the woman-without-eyes
outside Quitivac.   He wonders
why they won't say his country right:
Mey-heeko, don't they hear?
Biting a paper cylinder
like for oil changes he is
ochre in the sun
When you die, when you go down
to forever
you go to dance, amazing birth
you might look still

but you'll not be still;
your blood will pool, in rivers & lakes
under skin behind eyes
all vital organs increasing
sacks of cotija clotting & rising
you'll not be still but fly.
mauve fingernails like ribbons
eyebrows fattening bushes
arms to branches cells bursting open
ten thousand volcanoes, stars
off & on they crash ...
His mother tells him
something in a trio
of coded languages ... *flower of fire*
rushing the sun ...
terrible hopeful new days

& you will see that region of light
promised the dead
where all are brothers
none of us stripped
from one another
no escape our oneness.
in the end
there will none of us be withheld
don't you think, missus?

The difference between the pool guy
& the gardener
& why you want to f&%k one
& not so much the other
& it's racism

for karen

one is your fantasy
the other
your mother's nightmare
you want to f&%k one
but don't know the other's name.
one's your fantasy
the other your slum

the way water slicks off his net
an illusion between
air & plastic
& plastic & water
the way his OP's have the top notch undone
the way turquoise tubing
coils in the back of his truck like snake meat

the way his father sprang for his ride
after he flunked out of SC
the way the sun smears his forehead
& the sexy top-stretch before dick-flop
that soft place where short & curleys
drop where cockslung checks his body
where you see the centre of him
proof that from his ass
& the back of his legs
some unknown chunk slugs him into being.
in a sea of toxic maleness
this recognition makes things easier
like, you fucking hate men

but *snugdick* wielded by this kind of dumb
baloney sandwich regular no-choke guy
mitigates some important piece of male bullshit.
the tops of his Popeyes
the way he wears flip-flops
the way he stops out for lunch
the way you want coffee with him
sophisticated iced coffee
when your pretend husband's at work or dead
drunk in the living room seven rooms away.
the way you want to f&%k
the pool guy
cliché American dumb ass   /   f&%k
with his mind / suck his wad &
f&%k him again if you can
Tuesday 3 PM / glorious
reason to keep sheets clean.

the way one time you saw
what might've been his wife
in the passenger seat
side-eyed & muted sweatshirt
the way he brings a cooler
of water & beer
the way his clothes look like they grow grass
the way the rake scrapes concrete
makes a pearl handled *Schkkype* noise
like of birds
a child lost
repeating loss
the way you don't know from Guatemala
the way he's covered in your dirt
the way he looks burnt
schizophrenic bee keeper
way he looks Vietnam
way he looks sorry he came
way he seems bare minimum
janitor of the garden
way his stewardship leaves you cold
like your father

way there are no women in his profession
way he seems to know the landscape better than you
way he knows how to jump the back fence
guey you seem to be his nightmare
hanging out the window
blowing on your nails.

Sangre Ingrediente

Shoulders back
pictures like Seurat
here they come
— the vernissage.
early pink boiler plate
frocked marbled fuchsia
under-feathers
(it was going to be huge).
(or not).

Just what is it about performance art? *It was a severed head on a table Joanne*
some woman screaming Yoko Ono's fallopian tubes were the gunmetal wormhole
to G-d. Oh well L.A. would have gotten it.

What was that woman tryna say
how she had no stake
how she kept tryna find
a way through the keyhole
ended up
sun in her hands.
full set /   / mfa

but she brought it. some handful of soot / some Diamanda handful of soot /
against a wall / *what do you do?   I mean besides this, hon?* /

what if it's just a handful of soot?/
what if #metoo means
handful of soot?
what if mfa
means handful of soot?
what if museum /   publishing /
career / means hxxd fxxl of sxxt?

she pushed it / all the way up /
all the way through her Jay de Feo /
all the way / leaning head

against wall / all the way higher /
pushed the handful
til it burst / spilling diamonds
through all her cavities /
all of her / a cavity /
 But what was they /
 what was they /
 tryna say?

Leaning down
she listening in
drove all night
just to listen in
two hours one way
four hours back
it was no parking
but she made it in.

& some bleak lot, miles away after the revellers dropped their pants & hung up their
accents / a star slung among refuse / a sloe gin puddle / nameless for concrete.
Miracle. How that tear-down sang. Now. There was something. Later, shoes on the
floor like mother's before she wrote a ribbon across the DNA of the city rushing
songs out of darkness where no song was before.

Emergency Room

she was speaking Spanish
& all the tears in her spleen
were flying out / little kids running
one around the other / up-&-down
two phrases on a Rube Goldberg machine /
the plastic bag on her elbow
drained an open bladder to her *pantalones*
getting soaked in drabs but busy telling
so all she could do was shake a leg & keep spilling //
I mustered all the Spanish from the Nautilus within
a mother pushing a boulder off a child / mustered
to remember / in the DNA / the words /
was she lost / did someone hurt her /
was she supposed to have more children /
was it something about my children /
was she coming with news for us /
could anyone have that much grief
for anyone other than themselves //
& in the end it was all about a man

AUTUMN
Pipe Dream Planet

Red Car to infinity

Gather near my skirts & hush.   Now.
When I was a girl there were double
& triple & quadruple tracks
on the streets of Los Angeles.
They went far into the desert &
all the way to the beach & everywhere in between.
Not-to-say there weren't bus lanes & tram tracks
& automobiles as well because there were. But these tracks
belonged to little red & yellow trolleys
that chugged beside the rest of us motoring along.
They seemed like the missing link
between how our grandparents travelled in horse-drawn carriages
& us racing around in Packards & Chevrolets.
Hammered on sand & cement bars that ran through the middle
of the streets, the trolley tracks were laid-in beside gravel & tarmac
that rose in heat swirls in the sun.   Our Red Cars
dinged a sound   part whistle & part song   & we rode
to school over Santa Monica Blvd. & all the way to Boyle Heights,
down to the pier on Saturday night & out to Susie in San Berdoo.
The Red Cars clicked like ticker tape & buzzed your face
as they flew.   On trips west we found pink & black shells
& later Uncle Bob put them in the wall for the family mosaic.
Remember all those years on Mulholland!?   What I'm saying is
there was a time in Los Angeles when you could go places,
where the air smelled of fresh bread & salt water
& Swenson's Ice Cream & the Helms Bakery man &
the shining Red Car, not so long ago.
We listened to the Sons of the Pioneers
& went to Grauman's Chinese & even after
they took out the cinema organ
they piped carnival music between shows
so it still felt like the pictures.
When we were alone we'd hold a transistor radio
like a golden brick on our ear & switch to KMPC
& listen as voices spilled out. All the kids were tuned in
& it felt like a secret we held between us.
The flick of the transistor.   That breathing wheel.

You don't have any idea what I'm talking about
do you, sweetheart?

Hymnal

& there she was
on Broadway
between 49th
& 50th
& you know
what that means
even if you don't
know the city
you can still feel it
because the city
is everything.

& I hailed
Toni Morrison
& she said
You know
I am
& I said
Tell me
you didn't
win the Nobel Prize
for those stories
& she threw
her head
all around
& said
Girl, you know I did
& we laughed
& crossed each other
on the sidewalk.

& smiling
I kept
looking
back of me
how she was

going along
like you do
but then
I just kept
walking
til
I heard
quick steps
behind me
& I turned around.
& her face
was in my face
& she stopped
a second
to catch
her breath
& she told me
something
I'll never forget.

recipe for sweet cake with enemies

Make the sweet cake between you & your mother.
She smashes me in the face
& stole the land my grandmother left to me.
Make the sweet cake between you & your mother.
She did the exact same thing
to my family
that she cried & dragged her legs in the street for
when her mother did it to her.
Make the sweet cake between you & your mother.
She said things to me
not even
Name Brand bleach
can remove.
Make the sweet cake between you & your mother.
I throw up
walking to work
thinking about
her lessons.
Make the sweet cake between you & your mother.
How many more years
can this go on?
Make the sweet cake between you & your mother.
Some days
I remember
good things rough
white woman hands
covered in freckles
her hard work.
sometimes they smoothe
across some part
of my body
some part she blessed
some part,
some once a year scope
a righteous crop
a terraced place

she deigned
to let her eye bedeck.
someplace not
too brown
for her blue /
blue eyes.
Make the sweet cake between you & your mother.
bless the mother.
Forgive all shortcomings
& long-held beliefs.
Make the sweet cake between you & your mother.
Even alone. over dishes. even after she gone.
Water. suds
& water.

Amy Winehouse

if Amy Winehouse sang the James Bond theme song &
if her teeth were set-in her head just right &
if she didn't have that kernel of Coke
hanging off her nostril &
if her body'd been able to exist in a way
that she could eat food
& not feel she had to throw it up
for work /
to be heard /
to say / *please* /

if she could live &
sing her gift / her creed
& that was meaningful enough
instead of ghostdiving
unsung songs
& another name
on the list of girls
who can't navigate love
or transcend opportunity

home ways

sometimes I'm sitting around
watching an old movie
thinking about an egg salad sandwich
waiting for the kids to come home

it's one of those days we don't
have to go to work, the floors
mopped, laundries in the dryer cycle —
far in the distance
a gardener, but not too close.
it's Los Angeles,
even if it's the sad sequel.

sometimes we come up
around a curve
see the old oil derricks
in their forgotten scrub
something built in 1940
a place where perhaps
the Kizh sang
long ago

& I think about
moments, our
grand chapter headings —
our wedding day.
that long drive
with the sky
melting blue & white
all the way
to Seattle.
having a baby.
being at home —
knife against toast
sway & away
the sound of our simple river —
home.

But those grand things —
how did we do them
how did we ever go through them
did they go through us?
our shoestring.
our white cable in the window —
like a spider's faithful dna
spooling endless tethers.
& then
when the tungsten reaches an end
& we sit
with pages & voices & wonder —
could poetry even matter.

my daughter —
so afraid of white dwarves & red giants
calls us on a tour of the galaxy
from her seat at the dining room table —
reminds us of the smallness
of this universe
within so many universes
how it's a thousand fireflies
at a firefly convention
where we are

she says
most everything is utter darkness
a kind of darkness
you can't even know.
other darkness.
mama, did you hear?

unless they take you
around the galaxy
it's hard to understand
other darkness
& I think about fish
far down
in the dark.
& the lava

that bubbles up
& out
making pipe dreams
of earth.
pipe dream planet.
all fall down.
all Barbie dolls in heaven.
all Barbie dolls in the dirt.

desert girl — arms hanging — alive!

when I was a child & *The Herald Examiner*
legged-open on kitchen beams between
lamps & books & cream of wheat &
glass-brown beer bottles & the smudged elbows
of flea market men in faint smells of Listerine
& Doans pills with rice-pudding-cooling
on-the-counter of vanilla-lemon-1970s Los Angeles
my grandmother read aloud the story of the desert girl —
arms chopped & smeared with sand
walking out of the desert

her blood drowned the tarmac
as she fled the scene of the crime
rolled from the culvert
& clung to the side of the earth
on the highway —
alive like those gold-sleepers
of the *Twilight Zone*.
It was out somewhere, past San Bernardino
past civilization & back to railroads
& stagecoaches & people come from the East.
Our progenitors, those faces from the photo album —
stranger, etched names on the silver service —
Willis, McGee, portraits made in St. Joseph, Missouri
on their way West.
                    What could be worth so much
        to sleep for 1000 years!?
                    The hub-hooped black 1957 tub
        covered in a canvas tarp.
                    The glass cage chambers
        slumbering through centuries.
                    The skull & bone leavings
        of a too early crack —
                    this desert, this hope & oblivion
        eternally in one landscape.

did desert girl wake
in blue numbness
or did she never sleep —
consciousness beside her
like faith or stars
going by gascaps & jackrabbits
along the scrub & stem of the horizon

The first car she saw
was filled with girls & boys
farther & then beside her
horrified, her river of blood
& sanguine dress
& remnants of arms
above her.
see me
call on me
mother
(later she said she held her arms high
to keep her muscles from slipping out.)

but the boys & girls were too scared to stop
so desert girl walked for hours
til an old couple stopped & wrapped her
in beach towels & took her to the hospital
where they dug the grotto of her thighs
to harvest sinew to bring her arms half home,
to bring her all the way out of the desert.

& she lived to tell the tale.

my grandmother folded the paper
turned grandfather's morning sausage
& plated last night's T-bone
in her lemon-true kitchen.
the bone she said
is the best part.
Saved it just for you.
I sat with my grandparents
& cried for unknown girls

under the 7 o'clock bells
of the Church in Los Feliz.

three things

Woman what is woman

hair curled under - mornings thinking about food - hands brushing children - her children - other people's children - maker of children - loves to lie down - loves to be on her back - loves her reflection in water - loves to say love - loves to feel love - loves kittens & other small animals (not bugs) that press against her skin mimicking love - rages against hormonal incursions - rages against unwanted hands & looks. puny.

Man what is man

builds things - arranges things - moves small hands til they are big hands over things that are square - makes things that are square round - makes things that are round square - cries when alone - loves to turn away from a crowd grasping its phallus - loves to work its phallus 2 to 4 times a day alone or with others - loves to look at arms & legs & buildings it has made - loves thinking about buildings that are dreams-in-the-making with phallus in hand - loves warm slick phallus in hand - wants to eat - never wants release from eating or the partnership of hand & phallus - wants others to hold its phallus while it eats - likes to grab the middle of things - wants to put everything inside of it into the middle of everything else.   deadly.

Planet what is planet

i'm travelling on the road top speed - trying to get somewhere - other people are around but i shun them - they're just like me - legs & arms & cars we catamaran hating each other & the proximity of each other's bodies in cars & houses - all that roundness & warmth we hate & long for simultaneously - how much we hate it & never want it to end - we rage sleeping doddering til one day we stop

everything is in order - everything in perfect use - everything is in order - everything in perfect use - see this blouse - it fits perfectly - see this blouse - it fits perfectly - see this blouse - it fits perfectly - every button perfectly every curve perfectly every sleeve pocket partition parchment-backed portion - every joist & leaf - every knob every eye every zipper every stitch - fitting perfectly - every perfect panel - every tree lined vista everyday perfect

Wetb*ck Diario

On   Motherhood,   Artistry,   Invisibility,   Oblivion

I'm an American.   I saw the chance to make a buck & I grabbed it.   At night I bite my nails to the nub, ten beetroots running red, hoping it'll all work out.

On   being   alone

I am the mother of twins.   We work together, sing together.   At night I hear them talking in special tones, their darkened room, two beds foot to foot.   I'm an only child.   I kind - of - know what it's like not to be alone — but only obliquely — like turning a bevelled glass, watching cobalt ribbons fall together & apart.   Their dance ultimately comes to rest, but how it swayed in cohort.   Mostly it's me in the mirror / my favourite / the mirror within the mirror / a million pairs of legs /   so many soft faces saying, yes.

On   rejection

Sometimes I look at the lists.   Home computer, laptop, online outlets; wall of letters, of acquaintance, of near begging, of nailing notes to the communal door — a ponderous list — belt loop, wet rope in shallow tide. Foothold.   Firm hand.   Secure.   *Secure*.   Fuck - you - money.   Plans with no end.   A holiday in the desert.   //   Every day I write & every day someone who's turned their face to the same sun calling *yes, says no*   Everyday I try to find a place to show up.

On   honesty

To me, being a *Latinx* writer means I'm a wanderer, an apostle in a place I barely understand.   A borderland. Being *Latinx* means I'm home in the west.   Being *Latinx* means I'm passing.   Being *Latinx* means I'm White & European — an American — because if I was Nahuatl, or Mixtec, I'd just say that.   I don't know what percent of me is Mayflower, but I know my mother's skin is so white it shines blue.   I know we speak English & that I was sent to study in England.   I know the roads to the *Baja* are dangerous *Linda & all dust, don't go there, why would you?*   I know I have one Spanish ear.   The Nautilus.   I know the first words my father gave to me : *Mija y Caballo.*

The bee man of El Sereno

the bee man of el sereno
is moving on the earth //
old memory // sun graveyard //
elemental shapes & booms
a monolith
& groan on what we are //
a flutter on what we could be //
old recipe

like the way the car
used to ride //
baubling white line-roads
of Los Angeles //
dusty //
bright //
a light-terror // then
a mellow hum

let all be well //

I think of the bee man of El Sereno //
the way pavement
melts & rises //
what is that sweet steam
that energy //
the bee man wanders
certain streets //
the good things
of Los Angeles //
his good, old hands //
scooping honey
this belongs
to the shape of ritual
I call the bees
& the bees come home
I call with bells

& my bees
come across

the bee man
of el sereno
is moving
on the earth //
leaves & grasses
he leans his body
in sunlight //
his particular language
on the wind hints
at what the body
of a man
might be
on this earth

WINTER
The Long Trip Home

Grandfather swim

The night nurse
came in
even that last time
to wake him.
To push
at his
rivers
to lean
on his warm
streams
to constrict
the flow
of his blood
to chart him.

She came
with her trawler
dragged a
silver footed
hypodermic
across the stillness
of his arms
dipped her mercurial stick
into his tired mouth.

She asked
if he needed
anything.
He did not —
except for rest

that thing
she could not give him
before his long trip
home.

The birth

The ones on four legs
ran away.
Her screams
were a shock
even to her.

Though the mate
had mated
previously,
he too kept in the
outback.

When the little one
fell out
from between her legs,
she had no reason
to smile
& carry on with
all that laughing
like she did,
but she did it
anyway.

She picked him up;
brought
her mouth,
over his nose,
sucked out
the clog,
jettisoned red streams
from his nostrils
through
the flute
of her tongue
onto the earth.
She had no idea why she did it

but she did it anyway

She rolled over in the leaves
nestled her backside in the grass
& cupped him against her.

Stars were up

.

The watchers

Day 1

the clutch is the what you hold close to you
almost /   it is you
if anything was ever /
the clutch is what you grab
when the house lights up
candles on the water
that promised
all was okay /
sudden
& on the shaft
they light the whole night in red trenches /
the clutch is the mystery of the why the car goes /
who made these civilisations ?
the clutch is the last friend,
maybe the only friend /

I saw a deer drinking by the River
east of the Wyaconda,
saw four horses on a slanted hill
west of the Wyaconda /
phone service went out
& the sky was covered in ochre /
phone service went out
but the green trees went on
til they were stopped by yellow fields /
all
of a sudden
it gets dark. /

I thought I saw a baby elephant in the river
but it was just a large woman from the Midwest.

In a pond she brought her body out
covered in a layer of green algae

//
email keeps coming
names i don't re+member /

they say it's so & so's birthday
but i don't even know where my mama is
or if she is or does
if her body still drags on & on
anon   //
all the time
I was in New York I did the voice
but different
from the voice
in California
I was in New York
& the voice was lower
sure of itself
& I realiz'd
it must be
I'm close to 40

Nebraska

I saw an old white bus
hidden under trees
next to a ramshackle house /
saw horses feeding at a window sill   /
a tractor & a pickup crossed each other
like angry lovers /   north & south going Zaxes /
two Carmel skinn'd deer turned their heads
& looked the other way
as we trammel'd by /
a stand of broken
burn'd blackbody trees /
cattle running next to the train
near Watrous New Mexico /
Route 25 & a lone white horse
on an opposite fence / threw open the curtains
& knew it was the West /

Day 2

water has cut through red earth
New Mexico blears / yam faced baubles of land /
noses in bulbous red dust / signs the First Nations
made their homes in a side of Redcliff /
their work the work water can do /
windows / faces / crevices in caves /
water //   human hands make like the work of water/
we follow the water / try to do what water does //

Side-car

men who pontificate on railroad cars
like they're doing a stand-up routine
for people they don't know
who don't care /
loud men imagine
they do /
bc all people care about men /   .
regardless of race or age
their pontifications travel/
how can we stop this?   /

The junk heart of America //
buses piled on top of each other /
brave little toaster/
everywhere silos /
such we have made
to protect & store
our men & meal //
a silo in the heart of America /
Taking the train / there's no Hitchcock, just horses /
in ones or twos /
making their necks long towards the shrimp green shrubs /
gleaming grey breaklines /
/ I imagine a man
one arm rais'd

coming out of the landscape /
motioning towards the train /
I scream *stop the train*
& look for the emergency brake /
no one else can see
only I can save this man
out of the desert from a botched hit /
or is he a farmer lost /
a man lost in the world /
a survivor emergent
after a light plane
merged with the tree tops /
I scream *stop / halt the train /*
a man is coming

does the train pause /
lurch & groan
does anyone hear ?
& still
even my lead actor
is a man

Towards California

this is everything I know about the man on the train /
he *loves his family* /
/ *it's cost a lot of money to get this trip* /
he'll be *in Stockton on Saturday* /
/ he's calling *all the people he knows* /
primos /   tias /   friends /   keeps asking
/ *is the truck okay ?*   / *did you get the money ?* / *did you make money, angel ?* /
/ *angel, did you make money on this run ?*   / *meet me at the place in Stockton* /
/ *we can change the trucks* / *Alicia is coming* / *meet me* /
/ *bring that thing* / *you know what I'm talking about, right ?* /

/ he calls everyone tia /   mija /   mijita /   primo / because everyone
is interchangeably / familia /   as he is a mexican adult male /
/ he tells the people / *the children went to the graves of uncle y pops* /
cleaned the graves / *of abuelitos* /
/ he tells a man / *be in town* / *have it ready* /
/ he tells one woman /
/ *be in San Bernardino* / *5 minutes* /
on the platform / *to give money* / *for the children* / *to kiss them* /

/ this is everything I know about the man on the train /
I've not seen him
but he must be wiry /
he asks / *are these phones working ?* / *calls* / *keep getting dropped* /
it is vacation but he cannot stop /

/ maybe he is talking to no one /
maybe he has no plans /
/ maybe he is alone / like everyone else /
/ this is everything I know about the man on the train /

orchid bulb//fox blood//seafoam — a poultice

For 7 children who perished in ICE *detention*

Darlyn Cristabel Cordova-Valle
Jakelin Caal Maquín
Felipe Gomez Alonzo
Juan de Leon Gutiérrez
Wilmer Josué Ramírez Vásquez
Carlos Hernandez Vásquez
Mariee Juarez

You will not be forgotten   nor ever
though you return   to air and earth

you will be in the dawn again —
braided in our bread —
our ox bones will bear the need of you

the essential you

our leaves and trees will increase with you —
imbibe of you   —
our riverwater will increase   because of you

we will drink of you in night —
you — the remanded
the blighted, the swept
you   the medicine for our children
   though no star shattered to feed you
   in the tremor of your hour of need —

your mother's hands   //   a fury //   a cloud //
all fastness // to bring you over —
the eternal recurrence of your gift   //
your footprint — *your Smallfoot*
on the place // every desert

plant and eye will become you —
you will not be forgotten //   you —

your useful voice will sing in the desert again —
your *childcall* and *ghostwisdom* —
your strength to withstand real conquest —
your ancient battalion against bronze heavy hands —
a pressure sacrilegious   from outside you —
your strength to rebuild
the tower of our people —

over and again — your ironweed —
your night — your time under glass —

though your throat was closed
it will be the tributary —
the medicine of your veins will speak the healing —
your body will return the protection
of which you were robbed

your body the breakers
your body the rock
your body the breath
your body the night
your body the safety
your body the light
your body the tunnel of grass
your body the place
your body our coven
your body our wood
until you become everything

poem.   my father like a boat.

ghost-slip.
in   and   out   from shore   to distant star.
where   will   you   turn.
did   sea   meet   you   well
did you angle   chin   over shoulder
or   look   back   to   me
                          was I   your   other star
did   you   fish   with me
the   times   you   fished   *la Salina*   with Chalé
could you   see   me
on   the   face   of the   moon
or   the   palm   of   your   hand
or   sketch   me   out   of   ley   lines
or   see
impressions   of   me
on   pine   trees   how   they   intersect
with telephone lines   &   faces
of   women
porch   swings   all the supports
that keep the house   floating   on   land
did   you   see   me
underneath   the   house
when   you   called   your   dog
come   out   into   the   light
sweet   girl?

Pitaya   Roja
Latin: *Hylocereus*

          we walk
ancestor   shellways
      by   midnight   liquor   stores   /
                    Pitaya   roja
        passing   cars   of
                women   off-to-work
in desert cold
          Little   flame   head   /
little   drop   of   *La   Ribera*   /
            it's   said   in   heaven
                            they   talk   about   you
                        like   they   talk   about
                                            the   weather //
        on the street   they say your name
          like a reason   for living

aqui
        they show me
                    a leathery dollop
                    in   open   stalls   /
I throw my head
                    '*this* is what you mean!'

Pitaya   Roja
        I will never know you
            this way //
        revere you
        how the uncles do //
you   who   change   dirt
        to   wine
                    //   because   of   you
        we   come-in
to   silk
        your   leather   hair   //
            droplet of dog head
                    desert candy

open-eyed rock   //   soft rock   //   red eye
    miracle redbush-baby
        desert   ice   //
I will never know you

there's a story of the hylocereus   —
how she baubled on the milk of heaven
& tributaries of Orion's belt
how she scooped Vermilion sky
        & flashed sand craters
    & cinnabar
        birth canals
to deposit her delicacy
        like turtle eggs
in the rough
        at los barriles //
    she's flying   oh great mud-clod
    & bloody mouth

along the *Malecon*
we creep in heat and history —
    white stucco roads
        glance
            to the cemetery
    the end
        of all bees turning   —
            lived bodies —
                places we have leaned

instead of *Cempoalxóchitl*
or sunflowers
I leave *pitaya roja* — the redmouth rose
at the graves of my ancestors
        Flores Del Cabo   —   ojos   rojos —
    a few leather pears —
    for everything
    that can never be known

The DNA to preserve proved contrary
to capital gains

No more tears.   The place is sold, she told herself.
What had been a ferocious dream
from a hundred years away
outside a Cork tavern
a million moonbeams ago &
night after night walking home
with lads, few bob, her grandfather sailing away
& bringing it with him
beside his mother's folded lace, trailing
reels & jigs & candle light —
had been made in America.
With 40 dollars & his good wife withal
he came with dreams & filigree
ambition lathering the way.
He was young then, younger than the man himself
who walked the plank in this, his father's bar
long decades after the ground was split to build the place.
Halloran, McDaid, Daffey, Coons, all had wanted
a pub in the new world.
But only Hanlon had done it.
& now it was gone.
Useless to even remember the past.
She spent the afternoon insisting she move on
& forget about it.
Like a new Irish would.

Losing the gene to remember
hurts for awhile, like a nail
being wrenched out
of the body   —   but in this new century
it is for the best.
In the short time.

that way lies the future

We always had another guy on the side all along.   A guy we really loved, despite the old man who crossed the threshold every day on his way to death.   Always we were that whip-crack kind of teevee journalist, house on the hill, always, that other guy on the side of our minds who we loved & clung to.

The whole time we're surprised when we see it next day on the news, how it went off shining on the hill, with someone else's name attached; that's our house, our husband. Black panties or no.   Every day I was hungry & every day the addresses kept feeling fainter, in along the faces of the innocents who don't think like this, in ones & twos they wander, backpacks, sterling, holes in their shoes.   All along we were just trying to make snug money for pizza & a little peace of mind.   Shocked we sent our dreams ahead, that cry-in that edges somewhere in the evening   *are we awake, are we the one who takes notes from someone asleep*   Running we dip away from that too unreal moment in the dark.

>   *email keeps coming*
>   *names i don't re+member /*
>
>   *they say it's so & so's birthday*
>   *but i don't even know where my mama is*
>   *or if she is or does*
>
>   *if her body still drags on & on*
>   *anon   //*

how many horses /
    that side clear glassy eye /
    does it remember
    how they built the land
we go by them / on the land
no saddle /   we don't even say
    thank you /
a dog, a horse, a rat /
/ how many horses is a train ?

a man in dreams shouts on the night train
his father says *come on man, you're asleep*
he says dad dad / sorry   I was dreaming /
a dream on a train so personal
the womb tug of train body
a mama sloshing us
before we emerge
Chicagee, Milwaukee,
on our way
to the front porch
of other dreams.

even if they were faking that dream
that *crie de coeur*
someone in their orgasm
we don't want to see it
can't see it
or what the national wet dream is
yet we look around corners
every day
see faces in ecstasy
take our shooter to bed
make it our bride
bring it with us to the Mall of America
dance it around the metaphor
til it warms & reminds us
it was promised an Italian dinner /
a real Italian dinner.   So
we squire it to Minettas
order it beefsteak
& linguini.   & bc
it excuses itself
to put on lipstick
all along,
the whole marriage,
we thought it actually cared.
We travel
to that shiver /
Crystal on tablecloth
/ red Betty

shimmying to the bathroom /
we thought that
doll-up
was some kind of pushpin
in the Rand McNally
mapping a future
where someone could love us.

anaphora, litany, excess & absurdity —
— for we who are linked by grief

I   dispatch from the west

We're linked by grief
by overcoats & snow
by smells in mother's kitchen
& the absence of them
when she cannot come home
or ever again.
   We're linked by steps
   home, by buses & the feeling
   of paper between fingers
   by faces of children,
   occasional, fleet
   snug in our hands
   their soft eyes up
   all dawns of the universe.
      We're linked in the way we clink glasses
      look out of windows, palm fronds
      in the road after wind, tires screeching
      & the chance to begin again.
         linked in the way we hold our breath
         when babies cross the road
         the first time / the thousandth time
            linked by the way coughing lingers
            weeks on the body
               the way a man recedes
               walking down the road
               a tower
               a corner
               an angle of body
               part of the house
         some side of light
            is that him
            is that still him.
         a man going away

a lover becoming fainter
& smaller
until he becomes
the trees
 we're linked by laundry
 & gasoline & prayer
 by ocean voyages
 across time
 the dream of our father's
 father's father we never knew
 who lives in us
we are the house & the memory.

we're linked like the bees
in the constant work of their legacy —
 to hope without reason
 faith without coterie
 love without proof
 spirit with no evidence of smoke or fire
 to day with every recurring night
  bodies alone under rivers
  a boat coming into the harbour
  we go up alone together
  eternally together, forever

11 dispatch from the east

remember when they found Spalding Gray's body
in the East River   when the towers
stood   still standing
I'm going up he said —
all our people here and away

remember when there were carriages   up and down 5th Avenue
when one brownstone   held a whole family   & the employees
who made the machine work   remember before that
when the Lenape lived rightclose to the river   to the trees
— is there a ghost in the house
— in the country
is it just a memory   an old c.o.d.   *is there a ghost in this house*
in the collection of spirit   animals   ocean waves
iguanas   cactus tongues   belonging to each other
the addresses the same —   *all along the desert*
                                   maniacs leave water bottles
                                   filled with poison
                                   because they cannot remember
                                   the pilgrims are their brothers
                                   their lovers their own children recycled again —

                                   & again the maniacs refuse to remember —
                                   they leave poison out for themselves
                                   sure as rainbow follows rain & goodbye closes hello
                                   awakening in some farthermost dream —
                                   tomorrow

This is
a small handed truth —

Hold hands with me in dreams
& let us sing a while
some soft-strung words.

The treaty

My father was the first to see through the schemes of the white man.
Even though he married white. (To be white!)
He said,
      my son when I am gone
      you are chief of these people
                even though I adopted that white waitress' blue-eyed boy
                gave him my name, remember
                the one you never wanted?
                I wanted to be a white entrepreneur, hey yah hey yah.
Across the plains can you hear the voice of your father?
All men are weavers.
                I love you mija. I promise to take you to Spain when you're 15
                    500 years out   1500 years old.
                All the time I promise I'll take you to Spain.
Always remember your father never sold his country.
After you died papá, your brothers & sisters sold the land
    where tortugas slide onshore in the Baja
    they gave me your portion from the French hoteliers.
    much money y words I never knew,
    apostille seal, hectares.
      Always remember your father never sold his country.
He sold alcohol to pastel golfers from NBC Studios, Burbank, California.
You must stop your ears whenever you are asked to sign a treaty
selling your home.
Human, stop your ears when they iron you a treaty.
    The sound of burning parchment will travel with you like a bad relative.
      My son never forget these dying words, this country holds your father's body.
      Never sell the bones of your father & mother.
        I pressed my father's hand & told him
        I would protect his grave with my life.
His stepdaughter said   call the authorities
ask if the breathing tube of my father   could be removed.
Perhaps it was hurting him   they said.
I went to call, daughter of the bartender
& treaty makers   daughter of the turn down service providers.
When I came back to the room

to say
it is inhumane
to remove the breathing tube of a dying man
    my father was gone.
        I stood with the chaplain
        who saw I was my father's daughter amidst the golfers
        their loaves & handbags & hurry up eyes.
    The chaplain knew the truth.

    Why does it matter
    some stranger knows ?
    The Hague.   Always.
        A man who would not love his father's grave
        is worse than a wild animal.

(non-italicized words are from Chief Joseph, 1879 Address to Congress)

Post it from pandemic

I'm a contemporary of birds
of Donald Trump
of the lists
of the dead
on the internet.

strain to look.
        — our lady
        of the shawls
strain-in
on device.
   our knife
   oh mother
sharpening
eyes   in the sun.
        bail me out of here
        I chew stars
walk on stairs
   gender-less
   beyond hand touching.
        meet me
by tight memory
      some wet membrane
      stern break out room
   a kind of vinyl
   no virus can read.

wake me   lean & empty
   some close apartment   between
   father knees &
   gulfed marrowbones
     maps of
warm schlitz baths
all night.

there are fingers
in quarantine somewhere
some   fast body slam   & take away Chinese
for us sinners   ripped in open air

Bus lady

I knew a lady in North Hollywood
used to live
behind the metro station
in a car her brother left.
It had Minnesota plates,
the whole thing was a rundown.

After she lost it
she ran a scam
at Greyhound
on account of getting rolled
too many times
sleeping rough.

Every night
from wherever she was
she'd take a city bus
to Greyhound
& fall asleep in a swivel chair.
She'd have her suitcase at her feet
& one of those voucher sleeves
gripped in her fist.
Anyone walking by
would think
she was on her way —
with her neat hat
& lime green cardi.
But there was nothing
in that voucher jacket
just an empty pamphlet.

In the morning she'd
shuffle to the ladies
freshen up & be on her way.
By the time
she was back around

to that station
it'd been a couple of weeks.
She said
people thought
she was travelling fine.
If someone asked   —
Vegas or Reno
was always the guess
& right there
she'd make up a story
about nephews
around California   —
how every few weeks
they called for her
& how grandbabies
kept her on the move.
People thought
she was well-loved
waiting for her bus
to be announced.

After sleeping
in her swivel chair
she'd pad around town
go to Penney's
have coffee in the flute
at Farmer's Market
ride the RTD.
In the back of the bar
that summer we met
I'd seen her all over Venice
& she said there were two things
she thought about
nearing 70.

She missed
the old market
sitting out
among the stalls
with a big porcelain

cup of coffee.
She said wisdom
was hot coffee.
She missed
being young enough
to criss-cross the country
on her bus
& opened a pocketbook
showing an unblemished
handkerchief
that covered
her whole face in flowers
when she wiped
her chin.
She was Los Angeles.

Acknowledgements

We would like to thank the magazine & journal editors who first published these poems:

Raina J. Leon, Geoffrey Gatza, Jessica M. Wilson Cardenas, John McKiernan Gonzalez, William Jensen, Michele Raphael, David Lott, Roger Mitchell, Marcos McPeek Villatoro, Maria Miranda Maloney, Miah Jeffra, Yago Cura, and Cetywa Powell.

'If I was as smart as an onion skin' first appeared in *The Hudson Review*, 2010

'Springtime 1' was first published by The Los Angeles Poetry Society, 2017

'The refugees come like monarchs' first appeared in *The Acentos Review*, 2017

'Poetry is a shapeshifter' first appeared in *angels flight + literary west magazine*, 2017

'The saint of memory / the peas' first appeared in *Audemus* / Mount Saint Mary's Press, 2010

'Hymnal' first appeared in *Hymnal*, Mouthfeel Press, 2012

'Wetb*ck Diario' first appeared in *Foglifter*, 2018

'Grandfather swim' first appeared in *Underground Voices*, 2012

'Towards California / 100,000 bells of my heart' first appeared in *The Southwestern Literary Review*, 2018

'orchid bulb' first appeared in *Tlacuilx*, Hinchas Press, 2021

'The DNA to preserve proved contrary to capital gains' was first published by Blazevox, 2010

Thanks also goes to my editor, Cate Myddleton-Evans at Eyewear London / Black Spring Press, who shepherded this collection with such care.